People Management: Learn How To Connect

SADANAND PUJARI

Published by SADANAND PUJARI, 2024.

Table of Contents

Copyright 1

About 2

Introduction 3

Leadership Skills Training 5

Management Skills Training 23

Creating A Great Culture 42

Create High Performance Teams 62

Copyright

Copyright © 2024 by **SADANAND PUJARI**

All rights reserved. No part of this book may be reproduced, scanned, or distributed in any printed or electronic form without permission. Please do not participate in or encourage piracy of copyrighted materials in violation of the author's rights. Purchase only authorized editions.

People Management: Learn How To Connect

Learn Skills To Develop A Key Behavior, Connecting With Teams To Achieve Business Results

First Edition: Jun 2024

Book Design by **SADANAND PUJARI**

About

In our fast-moving, competitive world of jealousy, challenges and backstabbing, managers find it more and more difficult to control their workers and get the best out of them.

In some cases people are promoted to the position of managers without being given the adequate training. This leads to failure, or worse - their heart will fail before the failure comes.

During this time I have been able to help an eclectic mix of managers to make the right decisions and achieve success in their professional lives.

In this Book, I will teach you how to communicate effectively, both verbally and non-verbally, with your co-workers, your subordinates and your customers. When you communicate properly, you enhance the relationship and get the required results.

I will teach you how to manage your time effectively by delegating the right tasks to the right people at the right time.

There is no time to waste.

Enroll now and let's get started.

Introduction

Hi everybody and welcome to the advanced ideas chapter of the best leadership and management training Book. We broke this training down into four components: leadership management, business culture and teamwork. Those are your four key components that determine the success or the failure of any company and literally whether or not it is going to still be here five years from now. So what am I going to learn from this Book? Well you're about to discover one: what are the current leadership and management challenges that are literally destroying companies to specific tools, strategies and techniques that will make you an excellent manager or leader. Three multiple strategies for boosting employee performance that are so important for how to quickly take your company or your division to the next level five.

How to get the best results out of all your employees. 6 How to create and manage effective teams. 7 How to create a business culture where people actually love to come to work and give their all aid tools, strategies and techniques that will help your employees work at their highest level nine had dramatically increased employee retention. 10 how to recruit and train the best new employees. 11 has dramatically increased your performance and accelerated your career path. Twelve how to use teams to create amazing results, new ideas and massive profits. Now I put at the end here and much much more why because this is just a tiny fraction of what you're going to learn inside this Book. I promise you. So here's what you're gonna get within this training.

4

We're going to have an active combination of live chapters and we're also going to do our classic voice over PowerPoint interactive with dynamic slides, key information graphs, everything soup to nuts to help you become a great leader or a great manager. We want to have all the latest tools, tips , strategies and techniques to take your company and your career to the next level. We're also going to allow for some discussion time if staff isn't buying into the training they're not retaining the training and they're not carrying out this vision of how to proceed in the future. Then why even do the training discussion. Time is key. So without further ado I'll see you inside the training.

Leadership Skills Training

John Quincy Adams once said If your actions inspire others to dream more learn more do more and become more. You are a leader. Leadership is arguably the single most important value your organization can benefit from. But how do we incorporate it into our businesses and into our lives? How do we embody it in the workplace? And how do we develop it not only in ourselves but in those around us and below us as well. Because true leadership is not just about developing yourself or managing others it's about effecting positive growth and transformation in the people you work with. In this Book we're going to show you how to do exactly that so there's a crisis in leadership today.

Perhaps one of the greatest we've ever faced and it's all because of the leadership gap. You see 77 percent of companies are currently experiencing leadership shortfalls. With that number expected to rise to 84 percent in the coming year or so. What that means is that the older generation of leaders at various levels of the company ladder are getting old, they're retiring, they're moving on, they're dying and thanks to the demographic winter that the developed world has been cooking up for itself since the 1960s. Those leaders are not getting replaced by younger people fit for the job or rather they might be getting replaced but the Pickens kind of slim because for the most part it's gonna be millennials filling the gaps.

And I'm not here to bash millennials but they really haven't been getting shaped into leaders throughout their lives or careers. Leadership is simply a value that's been getting ignored for the last few decades both in business and in education. So not only do we have a situation where there's a smaller population of potential leaders to choose from but the ones who are there don't have the ideal level of leadership skills. In fact, in a recent study 63 percent of Millennials acknowledged they haven't been receiving the leadership development they need in order to face the challenge ahead for all the reasons above.

A whopping 89 percent of company executives insist that strengthening organizational leadership is a top priority and yet less than 5 percent of businesses have implemented leadership development at all levels of the small number of companies who do have leadership development initiatives. Only 10 percent of executives think that those initiatives have a clear impact on their businesses. That's right. A whopping 90 percent think they're ineffective to bring this dismal briefing to its conclusion. Fifty six percent of companies are not ready to meet their leadership needs and 71 percent don't believe their current leaders are capable of leading them into the future. Pretty bleak right.

Well don't throw the towel in just yet. There is some hope you see for companies that do have mature leadership development strategies. The number facing a leadership gap falls to just 49 percent. Now let's be clear. That's still a crisis but compared to that 77 percent across the board we mentioned earlier. That means that doing a good job of developing leaders can make a company 45 percent more likely to avoid the leadership gap and come out of this unprecedented crisis alive and well. So with that in mind let's dive into this training our Book is going to consist of a series of critical discussion points.

These are designed to cover this broad topic as thoroughly as possible to encourage growth in these vital areas and to facilitate a real and fruitful discussion within your organization about how you can each improve on these essential characteristics both at work and in your personal lives. Some of these will be pretty lengthy and some of these discussion points will be relatively straightforward and brief at the very end of this roadmap. The most important final step is discussion time. Do not skip this. This is the most important part of this training. When you finish this Book you need to spend at least an hour or so going over the questions we supply at the end as a group. Whoever is the head honcho in the group should designate a facilitator whose responsibility it is that each question is covered and that everyone.

Time permitting is able to have their say. Make sure all contributions are valued. All suggestions considered and all opinions respected. So let's move into the first discussion point led by example. Effective leadership involves showing not just telling if you want your employees to do what you want them to do then you should set the tone and demonstrate how it should be done. Excluding yourself from your own rules is a surefire way to lose your employees respect and make you unlikable. Practice What You Preach even if it's just for simple guidelines such as being professional or always being on time never stop improving.

Great leaders are constantly finding ways to improve themselves and find new skills in areas that they can learn and master. You should be open to the opportunities that come your way to achieve greater heights and pursue new possibilities. Prioritize growth and constantly challenge your team to be better versions of themselves and be goal oriented. Don't focus too much on the details and always keep the big picture in mind. Create a list of personal team and organizational goals and come up with a definite plan and strategy to achieve these goals. Direct your team's focus and energy into prioritizing urgent or crucial goals. These goals shouldn't be static.

Instead periodically evaluate them to adjust as needed. Keep in mind that when your goals and expectations are clearly defined your team members can better understand the end result that they're working towards as a unit. Furthermore it's easier to monitor progress and determine failures and successes. True leaders do whatever needs to be done. However when things go wrong you shouldn't point fingers or play the blame game. You should take responsibility for your team's actions and choices and their results. In doing this you'll show that you're worthy of your team's trust and respect nonetheless.

This doesn't mean that incompetent or reckless behavior from a team member should be swept under the rug. It just means that when mistakes happen you don't assign blame or offer up a scapegoat. Instead you identify the source of the problem and come up with a Book of action to correct the situation and prevent it from ever happening again. Decisive decisiveness refers to the ability to make decisions efficiently and to obtain a specific result. Leaders who are decisive decision makers appear more credible to their team members. A fast well-informed decision coupled with a sense of personal responsibility shows your confidence and effectiveness as a leader no matter what industry you belong in.

You're going to face difficult situations where quick and clear cut actions are necessary when it's time to decide. You should believe in your ability to guide your team to the right outcome and provide an impactful decision that aligns with your organization's goals and vision and give credit where it's due. Don't be that boss who takes all the credit for your team's success and hard work. Don't hog all the spotlight to yourself, be team oriented and give credit where it's due. Effective team leaders recognize that any situation, any success and achievement within the organization is a joint effort. Remember that no one wants to follow a selfish leader.

Furthermore it will be difficult for you to motivate your team when the next big project rolls around because they know that their contributions and talents won't get recognized. Being confident is not an easy thing to do. Some people are natural at looking at ease with themselves and their skills while others may require a little bit more effort. Have faith in yourself and your capabilities. And remember that you don't need to be loved or accepted by other people to be a good leader. Be authentic. Authenticity means being comfortable in your own skin. It's never a good idea to put on a fake persona or imitate leadership styles that don't really suit your natural personality.

Instead be proud of your true self. Draw from your personal values, strengths and experiences by standing up for who you really are. You inspire others to be the best versions of themselves. Engage in honest and open communication. One of the hallmarks of effective leadership as an honest and open line of communication with your team. Remember that it's crucial to be straightforward and ethical in your interactions especially when you expect your team to follow your example. Be flexible and change up your communication style depending on the team member or the situation. This also means you'll need to take the time to figure out which mode of communication each person prefers. You want to make sure that you are heard and understood.

But remember that communication is a two way street. Be a great listener and show that you're genuinely interested in what other people have to say. Be direct, transparent and honest and be consistent and constant with your communication. Remember that your team expects you to be there for them especially in difficult situations. So make yourself accessible and provide your team with several ways to contact you when they need help. Connect with your team members and find ways to connect with your team members and achieve a mutual sense of trust and respect. Having a real and personal connection with your team will create the trust that is crucial when ensuring accountability and boosting performance to create a genuine and positive connection with your team.

Take the time to learn more about their interests, their hobbies, preferences , strengths and weaknesses. These things will give you a deeper insight into their personal goals and motivation. Get in the trenches and spend time with the team to create a deep bond built on shared purpose. Encourage personal and professional growth. As a leader you should be invested in the growth and success of your team members. Provide them with opportunities that will improve their skills or help them learn new ones. Encourage them to do their best and be ready to take on challenges. Be ready to inspire and motivate. Remember that cheering your team on is a crucial aspect of being an effective leader.

Set aside a budget, even a small one dedicated to the professional and personal growth of your team. You can use this to organize training sessions, purchase leadership E Books and books or set up a mentorship program to help turn them into leaders by encouraging freedom, accountability and creativity. Mentor your team regularly and teach them how to be excellent in their tasks and determined to achieve their goals. Be positive as much as you want every day to go as you've planned. You're bound to encounter the occasional roadblock the way you handle an adverse situation speaks volumes for your leadership skills.

Research shows that when people are able to identify the good and any problematic situation they're better able to react with clarity and rationality before you come up with a solution to any kind of problem at work. Try to think of three positive things about the situation. This will reduce your stress and help you be more productive. A leader that focuses on solutions rather than problems is more likely to foster an engaged and productive team. A confident and enthusiastic outlook serves as a source of inspiration for your employees. Be receptive to new ideas. Change is inevitable and those who try to maintain the status quo will only get left behind and be receptive to the new ideas and perspectives that your team members bring to the table.

Change capable leaders drive innovation engagement and success. Encouraging your team members to provide their insights and ideas knowing that they have an active role in your decision making will make them feel more empowered and engaged. Take the time to talk to them one on one to get their suggestions on how certain things can be improved. You can also hold quarterly meetings to develop initiatives that can benefit the team and the organization. Keep learning. Effective leaders are the product of a never ending process of learning and development. You don't want to be the type of leader with outdated knowledge and strategies that are no longer applicable or relevant.

Don't be complacent and strive to learn something new every day about your team, your industry and the world. Work on your leadership skills by attending conferences or enrolling in Books. Don't be afraid to venture into uncharted territories. Visit other departments within the organization. Talk to other leaders within your network and get to know outside consultants that your company can employ. Read books, blogs and research reports. Participate in external industry events where you can learn about trends, discover new developments and solutions and expand your network. Empathetic leaders show compassion and care when you're able to empathize with their team members' feelings and situations.

You'll make them feel valued, respected and understood before you respond to a mistake. Put yourself in their shoes. Take some time to compose yourself and your thoughts come up with realistic deadlines and expectations. If it's something that you can't even accomplish yourself it might be time to rethink your decision. Recognize their work and efforts regularly and when you're reflecting on your actions or decisions. Try to visualize yourself as one of your own employees and ask yourself whether or not it inspires you to be more productive or perform better at work.

Share your vision. A clear and definite vision is essential to effective leadership. A clear vision will give your leadership direction and without it no one in the company will have a sense of purpose. If you don't already have one, create one of them that bodies your hopes, ideals and goals for your team and for the entire organization. Share this vision with your team members to guide them in their tasks and create in them a desire for growth and improvement by sharing with them your mental picture of the future. You make your plans more attainable and strengthen your commitment to achieving them. Manage your emotions. Great leaders know how to control their emotions because they understand that every reaction whether it's positive or negative will have an effect on their team and the overall success of the organization.

A leader who can't manage his emotions well can bring down morale and wreak havoc on the company's bottom line. Depersonalize issues don't take any of your team's actions personally. In fact it's almost never the case that the issue is about you never immediately responding to any feedback that you receive or problems that you encounter. Take the time to acknowledge it, assess what you're dealing with and come up with a list of possible actions or solutions to admit when you're wrong. A lot of people think that admitting that you're wrong means you're weak. However the opposite is actually true.

Nothing says strong and confident that having the ability to admit your mistake. Remember that being a leader is not about being right or perfect all the time.

It's about accountability. If you did or said something then you should be accountable for its results. Don't try to cover up or blame other people for your mistakes. Instead own up to what you did wrong and learn from it. It's a great opportunity to let your team know what you've learned. This is an effective way to build connection and trust. Learn how to spot talent. One of the most important aspects of good leadership is knowing how to identify the people who can move your vision forward. However hiring the right team members is just part of the process. You should also know how these people with their diverse backgrounds and abilities can work together harmoniously and effectively learn to recognize the strengths of your people.

When you do, you can then introduce strategies and plans to help them improve their existing skills, compensate for their weaknesses and grow in the best possible direction, support their development and encourage them to fight for their dreams and encourage independence and flexibility. Once you're certain that your team knows how to get the job done right. Stay out of their way. Remember that you hired these people because you believe in their capability to produce your desired results. Sometimes strategies don't work the way you want them to. Instead of getting frustrated over the situation, encourage your team to adapt and come up with something different.

Make sure that your people have all the support training and tools they need to make the right decisions. Cheer them on but step back and let them do their job. Trust in the fact that you've chosen smart capable people to handle it. There may be times when you'll have to step up and assist with tougher decisions especially when there's a struggle to reach a consensus. Learn to recognize these instances when your team needs a leader to choose the right path. Hold people accountable when you delegate tasks. You should make it clear that you have specific expectations and that you're holding the person accountable for results. Always follow up on your expectations after concluding a meeting with your team member immediately create a follow up date on your calendar.

Remember that if you don't follow up on expectations it sends a message that the task isn't important. Be consistent and don't implement a different set of rules for certain individuals or groups. Your team members should be accountable for both their actions and the consequences of these actions. For example maybe a salesperson is working hard and placing a lot of calls and that's great. But if they're not selling anything that's still a failure. And don't negotiate performance declines when people know that they can come to you to negotiate your expectations, standards , deadlines or goals. Be quick to praise.

Let people know when they've done good work promptly often and in public. You should definitely celebrate big successes together but you need to also acknowledge the small ones. Your employees must feel that their contributions no matter the size are helpful and valuable to the organization. However if your feedback is focused on constructive criticism or opportunities to grow and develop do it privately. Remember that no one wants to feel berated or admonished in public. Offer rewards and recognition. One of the best ways to make your team members feel happy and appreciated at work is to offer recognition and rewards. Come up with a reward system by asking your employees what they'd like to receive when they achieve certain goals or milestones. You might be surprised by some of their answers.

But this way you'll feel confident that you're giving them something they actually want. Don't send them standard messages of congratulations or appreciation. It's always better to make them personal and unique to each person. Treat the team to lunch every now and then even if nothing momentous has happened. It's an opportunity to know more about them and bond with the team, motivate and inspire. Simply telling your staff what they have to do is not enough. Getting them to be genuinely passionate about your strategies or ideas is what leadership is all about.

You should let them know your compelling reasons and motivations and make them understand how crucial their role is in executing the overall vision to constantly motivate and inspire your team members to engage, grow , innovate , be more productive and accomplish greater things. Remember that it's easy to force a subordinate to do what you want them to do. But getting them to rally around your vision is what will set you apart as an effective leader and encourage creativity. One of the most desirable characteristics for a leader is their ability to inspire intellectual stimulation. You should be able to encourage and drive your team to express their creativity at the same time. You should provide them with ample support and tools to come up with new and innovative ideas.

Encourage collaboration. When you brainstorm and work together you'll get more diverse and fresh perspectives on a project. Personal contact with other people helps unleash new and wild ideas, take risks and assign tasks to people who have never handled them before. Encourage them to find new and more effective ways to complete things. Ask your team for suggestions and recommendations about improving specific strategies or projects. Create a flexible workplace. If creativity is a big part of their job. Some employees work and think better when they're not tethered to a desk all day. Provide them with a separate space where they can clear their mind, relax or get inspired by a new scenery and be humble. Remember that humility is not a sign of weakness or a lack of confidence. Instead it shows inner strength.

Great leaders are confident about their skills but see no reason to constantly remind people of what they're capable of. Humble leaders inspire more respect and loyalty compared to those who bask in the glory all by themselves. While it's important to let your bosses know about your own contributions you should also acknowledge the efforts and hard work of your team and always put that front and center inconsistent leaders can cause a lot of frustration and problems. The people who work for them often spend so much time wondering how they should proceed or nursing grudges because they can't predict what their leader wants. inconsistency is thus not desirable because it reduces efficiency and lowers morale. Staying organized while having a goal or vision is important.

Coming up with definitive and clear cut ways to achieve those goals is just as crucial. Staying organized is key here. Always plan your day beforehand. List down every task according to priority and deadline. Make sure that you have enough time to deal with unexpected and urgent issues. Don't let your inbox run your day. Set aside specific times during the day to check and reply to your email. Make sure that your desk is clutter free. Remember that's your workspace. So if you want to get things done, keep the space available and respect people's time. Be realistic about the amount of time you give your team members to accomplish their tasks and do their jobs.

Remind them if they ever feel overwhelmed with the work you give them they can always ask for help from you or from their other team members. Start and end the meetings on time. Be specific about a deadline or a time limit when you say that something should be done by a certain date your employees should get it done by then. When you tell them that you need five minutes of their time you should only spend five minutes with them. If you're late or running behind schedule make sure that your team knows about it. Ask for feedback. Leadership involves constant improvement and in order to do this you have to know which areas you're lacking in to give your team the opportunity to give feedback about your leadership.

Having this kind of initiative demonstrates your willingness to learn and improve. Use anonymous feedback questionnaires so that people can be completely honest about their answers and be comfortable with conflict resolution workplace conflicts are unavoidable especially if you have a diverse staff. If you avoid addressing or resolving conflicts because you're uncomfortable, friction will continue to exist and it will eventually become too stressful for your team to work in the same place. Remember that you have resources that you can use to resolve conflict. This can be an H.R. staff or even a formal mediation process that's implemented within your organization. However you shouldn't just pass on the entire responsibility to H.R..

You should at the very least try to ask questions and remain neutral. Offer guidance and help each party see the conflict from the other's perspective and cultivate a diverse workplace. A diverse workplace fosters innovation. An organization that fails to embrace diversity condemns themselves to the same bias and narrow focus that they've been used to. There is no room for growth and development in an environment where all people have the same opinions or points of view. Team members who come from different cultures, backgrounds and perspectives can offer new skills and unique ways to approach a problem or situation.

As a leader you should always be respectful of people's opinions and be open to hearing differing points of view. Constantly reassess your leadership style strategies change over time. People mature technologies innovate an entire organization's growth and transform how leaders adapt and develop as one of the key factors that affect organizational change. Developing your leadership style involves applying your strengths within a dynamic environment and creatively motivating your people. However your style shouldn't be static as your organization changes so should your leadership style always adapt your current style to the demands of a specific situation.

Don't be afraid of failure. Failure is an opportunity to learn and a crucial step toward success. Remember that not all decisions you make will have a positive outcome. The key is not being right all the time. It's learning how to deal with failures and using them as motivation to achieve something greater. When you fail. Embrace it and don't run away from it. For instance if your project went over budget or if your team missed an important deadline don't dwell too long on your errors. Instead meet with your team. Identify the source of the problem and come up with a set of solutions that will help you avoid a similar fate in the future and encourage teamwork and collaboration. Any achievement from your company is the result of the combined efforts of all of its employees.

When you work together your team will feel as though they're part of something bigger than themselves. Come up with a clear and compelling goal or vision. Be clear about your expectations. Provide your team with well-defined lists of individual and collective roles and tasks. Make sure that the team is cohesive. Have a daily huddle where members discuss their tasks for the day. This will allow everybody to be on the same page and prevent competition or duplication of responsibilities. Encourage socialization outside of work. Organize team dinners, company outings and team building activities. These are great ways to break down any walls of prejudgment and encourage them to learn about their colleagues. Find a mentor.

Many leaders believe that they no longer need a mentor once they get to a certain point in their lives. However even the most successful leaders in the world acknowledge that the only way for them to grow is to seek the advice and guidance of more experienced mentors. A mentor will help provide a fair rational and objective perspective. Mentors have years of experience and insights that you can learn from. They can help you see and improve your strengths and work on your weaknesses. They can motivate and inspire you to be stronger, more confident and more decisive. They can expand your network and open doors for you in other companies, industries or professions and be more patient.

Don't overreact to the mistakes that your team makes every now and then. Instead, be more patient and compassionate and give them the benefit of the doubt. After all, nobody wants to or intentionally tries to fail. It's true that emotions can run high when failures are made but stay calm. Take a deep breath and take the time to figure out exactly what went wrong. Never be a source of negativity especially in high stress situations. Instead inspire them to be resilient and optimistic step up during times of crisis crises can happen and often are unavoidable both at work or at home. Being able to respond quickly and efficiently during these times of adversity demonstrates how good of a leader you are. When faced with stressful situations like these.

Step up and be the guiding light that your team needs. Don't see it as a setback. Consider it an opportunity. Since we know a crisis will come along every once in a while. Be prepared. Create a plan of action for every possible scenario you can think of and if possible. Practice them with your team. Be empathetic. In most cases simple and sincere apologies will often calm even the angriest customer or client. If you have to issue an apology as the leader it should come directly from you and not through the company's Web site or social media platforms let the effective parties know your sincerity and genuine regrets. Don't always play it safe.

Take some calculated risks that have potential for a big payoff and be honest and open with your team. You don't want your people to be left in the dark wondering what's happening or how they should feel. Keep them in the loop to reduce their speculation and anxiety about any given crisis. And finally be kind. Always emphasize the merits of kindness in the workplace. Kindness takes on numerous forms. It can be as simple as a smile or openly showing pride in someone else's success or accomplishments. Install a compliment box where people can write compliments, praises and positive words for their team members for every daily or weekly huddle.

Make sure you have something kind or encouraging to say, recognize and appreciate your employees regularly. A personal commendation from their boss will brighten up anyone's day and motivate them to work harder and perform better and now it's discussion time. The most important part of this training whoever is the head honcho in the group should designate a facilitator whose responsibility it is that each question you see on your screen is covered and then everyone time permitting is able to have their say. Make sure all contributions are valued. All suggestions considered and all opinions respected.

Management Skills Training

Henry Mintzberg once said management is above all a practice where art, science and craft meet. Becoming a good manager is perhaps one of the most difficult skill sets to develop consistently and apply on a day to day basis. That's because it's a practice made up of many disciplines. Sure, to be a good manager you need to be a good leader. That is you need to inspire, motivate and influence but you also need to have an excellent grasp of other things like planning budgeting, disciplining , delegating and countless more. The success or failure of your organization depends on your ability to skillfully balance at all. So there's no room for half heartedness and little room for failure.

In this Book we're going to help you with that leviathan of all life challenges. Being a good manager according to a study from Gallup 50 percent of employees quit their jobs because of their boss another online study by the Harris poll showed that 24 percent of employees would consider quitting if their managers don't provide adequate feedback while 68 percent of the respondents from a survey by clutch reported that they feel fulfilled when they receive accurate and consistent feedback our Book is going to consist of a series of critical discussion points. These are designed to cover this broad topic as thoroughly as possible to encourage growth in these vital areas and to facilitate a real and fruitful discussion within your organization about how you can each improve on this essential characteristic both at work and in your personal lives in general.

Some of these will be pretty lengthy and some will be relatively straightforward and brief at the end of this roadmap. The most important final step comes. Discussion time. Do not skip this. This is the most important part of this training. When you've finished this Book you need to spend at least an hour or so going over the questions we supply at the end as a group whoever is the head honcho in the group should designate a facilitator whose responsibility it is that each question is covered and that everyone. Time permitting is able to have their say. Make sure all contributions are valued.

All suggestions considered and all opinions respected so let's move into the first discussion point: get to know your employees on a professional and personal level, take the time to learn more about your employees including their career goals and personal interests. Get to know their relationships and passions outside of work that make them uniquely who they are. Knowing them as a person and not just as an employee will help you understand them more and leverage that information to help them succeed at work. Delegate some of your work. Many people who get promoted to managerial positions often try to do everything by themselves and take on more work.

However, effective managers understand the value of delegating assigned tasks and duties to your team members with the right set of skills and outlook to get the job done right and on time. If no one knows how to do the job, take some time to teach them. Your time is better spent on more important tasks instead of routine tasks that anyone else in your team can easily learn and accomplish. Lead by example, be a leader and not just a manager, turn your team's motivation towards a clear direction and goal. Show them how they can be successful within the organization by letting them learn from your example if you have high standards for your team work ethically and with integrity. Don't play favorites or single out specific employees for certain types of tasks or projects.

Cultivating trust by demonstrating that you also have the qualities that you want your team members to have to be an effective communicator communicating with your team members is one of the most important skills that you need to know as a manager. It's impossible to lead and manage a team effectively. If you can't motivate people, make them understand your vision or provide feedback properly. Here are some tips to help improve your communication style: prepare your points beforehand and practice saying them out loud, set clear expectations and specific due dates.

Don't make your employees read between the lines, always keep your team updated with what's happening in the company and any future plans. Your transparency will foster an inclusive culture where they won't be afraid to voice their concerns, opinions and ideas, be open to discussions and encourage original thinking and creativity and learn how to listen. Leading requires learning and learning involves listening. As a manager you should never make your employees feel that they don't have the ability to speak their opinion or contribute to positive change in the organization when you listen and let your team members express themselves.

You show your respect for them and also gain deeper insights. Following are some tips to help you listen well and keep an open mind. Effective listening skills involve five components: understanding, remembering , assessing and responding. Go through these components one by one whenever you're talking to an employee. Be attentive , maintain eye contact, take notes when necessary and wait for them to finish before you start talking. Let go of your preconceived notions and don't jump to conclusions before or during the conversation. Listen with the goal of knowing as much as you can about the situation.

Prepare for discussions and meetings but never assume that you know what your employees are thinking what the problem is or what the solution is acknowledge success celebrate the success of your team recognize their achievements and let them know how they were able to contribute positively to the organization don't get hung up on what's missing or what they weren't able to accomplish and focus instead on their hard work according to a study by the Harvard Business Review. High performing teams have a ratio of six positive comments to every one negative criticism. Praise is a powerful motivator and sometimes it can even be better than money it makes.

Employees know that they did well and encourage them to do even better in the future to motivate your team. The ability to motivate other people is one of the most desirable traits for any manager. Your team members should have a positive belief in the ideas and tasks that you are asking them to do. They shouldn't think that these tasks will bring about second rate results when the atmosphere at work is positive. Morale and productivity will also increase. Here are some things that you can try to motivate your team. Make sure that each member of your team understands their role. Provide your employees with a clear set of goals and an understanding of how to attain them ensure that they have the facilities and tools to ensure that goals are reached on time.

Monitor their milestones along the way. Figure out what motivates your team members. Do they prefer continuous feedback and quiet appreciation? More challenging projects or external recognition. Make sure that they are paid what they're worth. You don't want to lose high performing team members because they're being underpaid. Encourage collaboration and teamwork so that each one feels like they rely on the team for support and assistance. This will instill in them a greater attachment to the successes of your team and the company exercise restraint. It's easy to let the stress at work get the best of you.

You might be tempted to let out your frustrations on your employees but remember that you'll have to deal with unmotivated employees who will be ready to leave at the first chance they get rein in your temper, stay calm and think things through. If you were an employee you also wouldn't be happy to work at a place where the manager gets easily provoked and always has something unpleasant to say practice a little patience and instead of flying off the handle right away listen patiently to the issue at hand and offer sound advice and support practice self reflection effective leaders are self-aware.

It's impossible to manage other people when you can't even manage yourself. Set aside some time to reflect on your actions, reactions and future initiatives. This can come in many forms including regular counseling sessions with your boss researching various leadership techniques or asking your peers about how you can improve. Remember that you shouldn't be so focused on other people that you forget about yourself. Calm down, consider your strengths and weaknesses and identify a Book of action to help improve those areas you need to work on to set clear goals and deliverables. Goal setting is one of the hallmarks of effective managers.

You need to have a clear vision and strategy for your team. Clear and well-defined goals will not just serve as a roadmap for the work that needs to be done but will engender a shared sense of purpose in your staff. When creating the goals for your team keep the following in mind: each goal should be linked to a set of deliverables which are essentially small actionable tasks. Deliverables will help your employees better visualize how their individual contributions tie into the bigger goals of the organization. Make sure to reiterate these goals and deliverables at every milestone. Monitor their progress to ensure that things stay on track, schedule one on one meetings where you can give them advice on handling certain tasks or situations, avoid ambiguous wording and set SMART goals that get constantly updated and evaluated.

Holding your team members accountable does not just involve holding your subordinates responsible for their work and their actions instead. Accountability must flow in all directions within the organization. Each member of the organization should hold one another accountable including those in the upper ranks if you want to hold your team accountable to their tasks. Make sure that you communicate this as clearly as possible. List down the expected outcomes completion dates and any other detail that they should pay attention to measure results with correct and comprehensive data. That is also available to the rest of the team. Be inclusive and encourage all of your team members to contribute to reaching the team's target.

Don't just rely on certain people to accomplish the most crucial tasks. You don't want to exclude your employees from tasks that they may also be qualified and skilled enough to do before you allocate work. Make sure that you take into account their opinions and ideas. Don't just hand out instructions to your team members without obtaining their feedback or letting them understand what the task entails. Even the newest member of your team may prove to have a very useful or insightful suggestion to create a collaborative environment. A collaborative environment is one where all the members of the team feel respected and valued. You can achieve a collaborative workplace by letting your subordinates see your own passion and positivity for your work.

At the same time don't try to do all the work. Instead delegate and encourage communication through feedback and regular one on one meetings. Make sure that you emphasize the importance of a welcoming and supportive atmosphere at work. Define success success can be defined qualitatively or quantitatively. The former is measured by observations and focuses more on soft skills such as flexibility, communication or teamwork. The latter is measured by metrics or statistics for every project that you take on as a team. It's important for you to assess your team's performance through both types of measurements. Quantitative performance evaluations are impartial and objective and are specifically designed for the employee's role.

Some of your team members may be more receptive to seeing the outcomes of their work in black and white. On the other hand, qualitative performance evaluations are ideal for roles where success can be a little more abstract. Managing behavior might sound like something out of a kindergarten teacher's list of tasks but effective managers understand its importance in the organization. As a manager you want to be certain that your employees behave in a way that aligns with the organization's values and company culture. It is your job to make sure that your team members understand the importance of your company values and that compromising these values is never in their best interest.

Managing employee behavior will also help you create a productive and effective workplace that will ultimately drive your organization ahead of the competition take a leadership Book Leaders aren't born they're made actively working on improving your leadership skills will make you a more effective manager however it's tough to improve on your own and sometimes it's better to ask for expert advice and assistance one way to do this is to enroll in a leadership training program. There are various Books that will make this process easier for you. Some of them are free although the more popular ones are offered at affordable rates. They include Books on critical thinking, decision making, how to create change and how to disagree.

Properly be transparent. According to the American Psychological Association approximately 25 percent of employees don't trust their employers. As a manager you don't want employees who don't trust you or the company since they are unlikely to align their own personal goals with that of the company. Here are some great tips that you can use to promote transparency at work. If there are any roadblocks that they may encounter during the Book of their work let them know about it. Offer suggestions as well on how they can handle these roadblocks if you received vital but not confidential information from senior leadership.

Make sure that your team knows about it as well as explain the rationale behind your decisions so that they are not left wondering about your reasons and motivations. Don't be afraid to be the bearer of bad news. It's definitely not a pleasant experience but your team members should know about both the good and the bad. To help them adjust and improve continuously, create a feedback system and implement a system where your team members can give you feedback on the work that they are doing. Timely and consistent feedback from your subordinates will help you identify weaknesses or adverse behavior as well as reinforce positive ones. Your employee should know that they are free to express themselves when they feel that something's wrong.

You can try holding one on one meetings or an anonymous suggestion box where your team members can let you know how you are doing as their leader balanced praise and criticism. Your team members need a healthy balance of praise and criticism in order to succeed in their roles. If you only provide praise you're not really helping your employees grow. However if you only offer criticism your employees will get demoralized and be constantly on edge. Try the following tips if you were developing a system for providing constructive comments that give more praise than criticism. Research from the Harvard Business Review showed that top performing teams typically have a constant and continuous flow of positive comments never lie to your team members about how they're doing.

Figure out when, where and how to give praise properly, good results and behavior should be acknowledged and rewarded consistently and promptly. Remember that public and private praise as well as special recognitions are great management tools for building trust and morale. Criticism must also be timely. However you shouldn't just identify their mistakes, provide them with feedback that will help them overcome their weaknesses by allowing them to set goals for improvement. You are demonstrating your belief in their abilities and skills. Always finish on a positive note. Be specific when commenting on their work instead of just telling them that they're doing a good job.

Mention a specific project and let them know why their actions or efforts were commendable, provide mentorship or career development opportunities to raise morale and motivate your team to achieve greater heights. Your employees have to feel that they are growing in their roles and learning new things. They should be able to see short and long term career opportunities that will enable them to reach their full potential. Otherwise they'll most likely be looking for better opportunities elsewhere and take the time to create development opportunities that would help each staff member progress on their individual career paths.

If you don't have the budget for large scale conferences or trainings consider getting more senior employees in the organization to mentor your team members and help with their career goals use stretch assignments to challenge your team a stretch assignment is one that involves skills or knowledge that is beyond the current repertoire of an employee to help your team members learn new skills and help them handle work outside of their comfort zone. Try assigning stretch assignments every now and then. Here are some of the top reasons to use stretch assignments to determine whether or not an employee has the potential to take on leadership roles and more responsibilities.

Prepare your team to step up when you are not around test new ideas concepts and approaches ensure that you'll have manpower if the organization decides to expand into new programs and projects expose your team to other departments and areas of the organization don't micromanage micromanaging occurs when managers try to personally control every aspect of a staff members work. This often means that the manager will lose track of the bigger picture and focus too much on the details. Micromanagement is counterintuitive and demoralizing because your employees won't have any freedom to think for themselves and make independent decisions. Here are some of the dangers of micromanagement When you drastically limit your management style.

You also limit your means of communication and ultimately your management ability your employees lose their trust in you they'll no longer see you as a manager but as someone who instills fear and anxiety your employees will lose the confidence to complete tasks on their own and instead become heavily dependent on you and your constant interference you'll quickly burn out micromanagement is exhausting and the work will eventually get to you. It may even cause you to hate your job and even the organization that employs you create an employee recognition system being held in high esteem by your peers motivates an employee to work harder and makes them feel that they are a great fit for the organization and employee recognition system acknowledges the contributions of a staff member to the goals of the company and commends their exemplary performance if you are planning to develop a recognition system for your own team.

Here are some cool ideas that you can try out: monetary bonuses will always make an employee feel valued because it shows that their hard work is paying off. Custom gifts or company branded items such as bags, tumblers or shirts to employees who are performing well, schedule a free lunch for your team to treat them for doing a great job for the week, celebrate work anniversaries, birthdays and other significant life events with your team members. Make sure that everyone's eligible for the recognition don't exclude anyone or any group especially if you manage a team with varying responsibilities. You may want to consider creating multiple recognition programs for different types of roles or positions to make work more fun.

Some of the most successful companies in the world have created a workplace where employees can stay happy and motivated. Make sure that you find the right balance so that while they can have a place to clear their minds and feel refreshed they are still able to stay engaged and productive. Following are some great ideas to make your office more fun and have a small recreational area. Consider adding a couch, some beanbags, a picnic bench or a pool table. This will serve as a place where your employees can stay if they need a break or wish to relieve stress. They can also take their laptops with them if they want a change of scenery away from their desks. Organize nights out so that your team members can get to know each other better and form friendships outside of work that can encourage collaboration.

Back in the office your office should also reflect your brand, decorate the place and make sure that it's attractive and interesting while also staying on brand. A study from The Economist reported that having a dog in the office can boost productivity and reduce stress. Working with a dog nearby also encourages employees to become better collaborators, admit your mistakes, true leaders know when to show humility and admit their mistakes by letting others know that you are not perfect.

You earned the respect of your employees and brought yourself closer to your team. Furthermore it helps instill loyalty in you admitting your mistakes also demonstrates the strength of your character and encourages your team members to not feel embarrassed to admit any mistakes that they may make in the future refine your decision making using sound judgment and making wise decisions is one of the hallmarks of being a good manager instead of focusing on the outcomes of your choice. You might want to take a look at the way you come up with a specific Book of action an effective decision making process involves the following elements quality requires analyzing the problem and comparing the options that are available to you execute ability involves ensuring that your team is on board with the option that you have chosen to boost the likelihood that your decision will be executed properly and create positive outcomes timeliness means ensuring that your decision is implemented at the right time.

Empathetic empathy refers to the ability to understand someone's situation using that same person's perspective. Being an empathetic manager helps you become more tolerant of diverse ideas and opinions helps develop trust and long lasting relationships and be more open to change. Here are some of the top reasons for you to learn to be more empathetic in the workplace. You can easily recognize the feelings of your employees and control your actions accordingly. You are more motivated to follow a strong moral compass built on communication, kindness , respect and tolerance. You'll think more about the needs of your team members before you make decisions and you'll be more calm and accepting of criticism.

You won't get defensive or argumentative in high stress situations you'll be more willing to take risks for the team because you value character over your ego learned to separate personal problems from organization problems if you have built a trusting relationship with your employees they are going to come to you when they have problems however you shouldn't treat these problems equally. Understanding the difference between personal and an organizational problem will help you come up with an effective response. You can correct personal problems through your people management skills without requiring considerable reorganization. On the other hand organization problems are caused by inherent issues within the organization.

You'll need to take control of the situation. Talk to the senior leaders about possible solutions in keeping your staff's head above water until the issue is completely resolved check in regularly even when there's nothing wrong. Make sure that your employees are able to easily approach you when they come across any problem or issue at work and check in with them periodically but don't pop in or hover around so much that it becomes stressful or awkward in this way. You can quickly put out fires before they turn massive. Regular one on one meetings are also ideal so that you can check in on their progress as well as get to know them better. Encourage your employees to be problem solvers.

At one point or another your team will encounter seemingly impossible situations. They'll walk into your office and leave things up to you. This isn't how it should be done. Your role is to boost efficiency, not add on more to your plate as their manager. You should encourage them to come up with possible solutions before they come to you for help. Following are some ways to help you encourage problem solving abilities within your team. Provide them with sufficient tools, freedom and responsibility to fix the problems that come their way and trust them to get the job done. Don't let them become dependent. By not micromanaging constantly looking over their shoulder or always bailing them out, set goals instead of giving them a list of instructions.

Letting them figure out how to complete the job instead of giving a sequence of steps that they can follow encourages creativity because some problems don't always require a linear and logical way of thinking that facilitates brainstorming. Teamwork is always a good thing. If there is a problem that your employee can't solve on his own try letting him work together with a group get better at identifying talents delegating tasks requires having a solid grasp of your team's talent pool you should be able to recognize your staff's skills and talents and harness them in such a way that would benefit the entire organization. Remember that not everyone can handle certain tasks capably or easily so you should identify each member's strengths and weaknesses.

This will then help you create and allocate the tasks better and organize the workflow more efficiently to give people autonomy. It can be tempting to just tell your employees exactly what you want them to do. This can work in situations where the employees are unable to meet your expected quality of work. However most employees prefer being independent and like to be challenged. Allow your employees to take responsibility and accountability for their work. Here are some ways to encourage autonomy with your team members, challenge them but make sure that they don't get overwhelmed and establish boundaries while autonomy is generally a good thing. Too much choice can also be dangerous.

Let your employees be autonomous but also hold them accountable for the results and create opportunities for your team to learn about organizing, balancing priorities and goal setting autonomy does not mean completely abandoning them.

Make sure that you are always there to offer advice and support and don't sweep problems under the rug. Whenever you encounter problems within the team or the organization don't tiptoe around them. Instead face them head on and never hesitate to take a step forward and come up with possible solutions before it adversely affects your team. Keep in mind that an aversion to uncomfortable situations shouldn't keep you from fighting for your team and looking out for any problem that might threaten their well-being and quality of work.

Your employees want you to stand up for them so that they can do their jobs to the standards you've set. Be receptive to negative feedback and don't react defensively if you receive negative feedback. In fact always assume that the person who gave this has a good intention. It's basically the same thing as providing feedback and criticism to any member of your team that isn't performing well. You want them to learn and improve in the same way that they want you to help them change things. If no one in your team wants to come forward with an honest criticism. Change your approach instead of asking for feedback. Ask them for advice. Sometimes people see the word feedback with negative lenses.

It can seem too formal or forced. Asking your team for advice demonstrates your belief in their knowledge and skills to handle toxic employees. Even the best managers can get saddled with that one employee that makes work life miserable for the people around them if you can't let him go immediately. Here are some great ways to respond to their behavior and reduce the damage they cause: identify the cause of their discontent or are they unhappy with their role or are they experiencing adversities in their personal life. Meet with them to find out what their reason is and offer to help make sure that you let them know directly the effect they have on the rest of their team.

Toxic People can be oblivious to their surroundings since they are too focused on themselves and their issues schedule one on one meetings with the rest of the team to get the other side of the story develop a plan of action to address the situation if the toxic employee is still resistant to change accept the fact that you won't be able to fix things and explore other options. Document the behavior and the steps you have taken. Any official warnings you have issued and the complaints from the rest of the team always are on time even if you are just meeting informally with your team members. Stick to the agreed upon schedule. This shows that you respect their time as highly as you value yours. It will also help promote trust and respect in each other.

If you are regularly late to your team meetings perhaps it's time to take a look at your time management skills. Even if you have to cut a previous meeting short, show up on time. If you know that you are going to be late. Make sure that you inform them at least an hour beforehand to prioritize health and well-being. Healthy employees are contributing employees. Studies show that one of the biggest sources of inefficiency and productivity loss are sick employees. Make sure that you encourage your employees to take some downtime every now and then to distress and rejuvenate lead by example through taking your holidays, prioritizing downtime and putting your health first. Remember that you should never give your employees the idea that working 24/7 is the only way they can achieve success in the organization and manage expectations. Sometimes clients and superiors will push for outcomes and deadlines that are just not feasible.

In cases like this let your bosses know what your team is realistically capable of accomplishing given their desired outcome an existing workload give them a more attainable picture letting your superiors know when something is not reasonable would help them adjust their expectations or at the very least provide you with tools and resources that you can use to work faster and more efficiently and now it's discussion time. The most important part of this training whoever is the head honcho in the group should designate a facilitator whose responsibility it is that each of the questions you see on your screen is covered and that everyone. Time permitting is able to have their say. Make sure all contributions are valued. All suggestions considered and all opinions respected.

Creating A Great Culture

Brian Christopher Coke once said being a great place to work is the difference between being a good company and a great company. The success of your business is largely dependent on your company culture. The atmosphere of your workplace, the traditions, the routines, the values all have an undeniable effect on the performance of your teams. The morale of your workers and even your bottom line. So what can you do to foster a positive company culture? How do you ensure that when your people show up in the morning they're both happy and proud to be there.

Well in this Book we're going to show you how to do exactly that 94 percent of executives and 88 percent of employees believe that a well-defined workplace culture is important to the success of a company 46 percent of job seekers believe that company culture is an important consideration when deciding to apply to a company and 15 percent of job seekers turned down a job offer because of a disappointing company culture based on these statistics. It is clear that a positive company culture is something that your company should strive for. Our Book is going to consist of a series of critical discussion points.

These are designed to cover this broad topic as thoroughly as possible to encourage growth in these vital areas and to facilitate a real and fruitful discussion within your organization about how you can each improve on this essential characteristic both at work and in your personal lives in general. Some of these will be pretty lengthy and some will be relatively straightforward and brief at the very end of this roadmap. The most important final step is discussion time. Do not skip this. This is the most important part of this training. When you finish this Book you need to spend at least an hour or so going over the questions we supply at the end.

As a group whoever is the head honcho in the group should designate a facilitator whose responsibility it is that each question is covered and that everyone. Time permitting is able to have their say. Make sure all contributions are valued. All suggestions considered and all opinions respected. So let's move on to the first discussion point: assess your current culture. Building a company culture from scratch is easy when you're just starting out. After all, culture starts with the very person you hire; their set of beliefs and values will help dictate the kind of culture that will develop. However if you already have an established organization or company you'll need to assess and redefine your company culture.

If you want to see some improvements here are some simple steps to understand change and improve your existing company culture. Evaluate your onboarding process. If you're hiring and training methods they're antiquated. Consider transitioning into more personalized and participatory processes to determine whether the leadership is fluid and agile. Change won't happen if the company leaders are static and resistant to change. Look at the company's recognition and rewards program. Give employees several options on how they want to be recognized and rewarded by observing the interactions and dynamics between teams.

The goal is to establish strong connections that will pave the way for effective collaboration and define your values. Make sure that you know and identify the values that underpin your business operations. Otherwise it won't be easy for you to determine what you want your company culture to look like. Some examples of questions that you should ask yourself when defining your company values are the following. Why does your company exist but does your company stand for. What is your mission or vision? Where do you see yourself and your company? A few years down the road how can the employees demonstrate these company values.

Why do the company values matter and how can they contribute to individual and team success? Institutionalize the culture. After you've identified the kind of culture that you want to have in your company the next step is to create and implement new systems and standard operating procedures. These policies and processes should reinforce the existence of the new culture. Furthermore they must be scalable and easily accommodate the growth of your company. Here are some ways to encourage the permanence of a new company culture. During the hiring process. Give multiple employees the chance to assess whether or not a potential hire is a good fit.

During performance conversations make sure that the company values are an important consideration. Have your values placed front and center on the company website to help attract the kind of employees who would be a great fit with your company culture. Consider adding the company values to employee email signatures. This creates a shared language and signals to the rest of the world that the employees embody these values build trust.

The foundation of every good company culture is employee trust. It is unfortunate that a lot of larger corporations experience an increasing sense of alienation and distrust between their employees and leaders.

Communication issues are often the culprit as managers in these bigger companies don't get the chance to know all the employees and develop a closer, more personal relationship. Good communication is always the key for building trust. Communication lines can be improved by making time for one on one meetings providing employees with autonomy and accountability and making them feel valued and appreciated. Get employees involved. It is true that culture change should come from and be modeled from the top. Leaders should pioneer changes in company values and goals in order to ensure actual transformations. However the role of the average employee shouldn't be diminished.

Diverse perspectives should have a voice in creating the ideal company culture. Encourage employees to share their recommendations comments and ideas share the responsibility especially when it comes to onboarding new personalities that will eventually have a significant impact on existing practices and values emphasize organizational hierarchy organizational hierarchies can be limiting and repressive particularly when there is a lack of transparency or accountability in the leadership hierarchies can make anyone feel intimidated. They also restrict the free flow of ideas and creativity adversely impacting organization development.

Instead of focusing on structural differences, create positive workspaces without the inherent division that hierarchies bring each employee should feel heard, recognized and valued. Office politics should be discouraged and gossip backbiting or politicking should be prohibited. Reduce bureaucracy and micromanagement in many smaller businesses. The need for organizational hierarchies can actually be eliminated. A flat and open organizational model can work when there are too few employees to require the need for middle managers. This kind of structure also eliminates bureaucracy.

Since employees now have direct access to their managers or business owners, furthermore never micromanage your team members to make all of them feel like they belong and that they are capable of handling and finishing their own work. When employees own their work they feel valued and have a better sense of belonging. Optimizing the hiring process company culture is directly influenced by hiring decisions. Taking your time to hire and promote the right people will pay off and make a difference in how your company will ultimately grow. Getting the hiring process wrong is palpable and will eventually manifest in problems for the company.

Here are some tips to keep in mind during the hiring process to cover as much ground as possible by assigning your team different areas of the interview. When you have multiple interviewers covering different subjects you'll get deeper conversations and a more comprehensive picture of each candidate's attitude should be prioritized over skills and experience. Ask them if they plan on growing with you even if the position or task you have hired them for is gone. They should be genuinely excited not just with their role but also about being a part of the company. A great culture fit doesn't mean someone who looks, thinks or acts like you or the rest of your team.

Instead, find someone who brings something new and exciting to the table but will also align well with your company's values and vision to build a strong employer brand. An employer brand refers to what employees think, feel and share about the company they work for. Essentially it is a company's reputation as an employer. Unfortunately not a lot of companies pay attention to their employer brand let alone invest in building and strengthening it. Remember that a strong employer brand helps attract and retain high quality workers. This is what will differentiate you from your competitors.

Although there is no one size fits all solution for improving your employer brand, you should invest in creating a healthy work culture that creates happy and engaged employees. One of the best ways to create a positive company culture is an engaged work environment where employees clearly see that the management cares about them and their future. Invest in your workforce and allow them to pursue their passions both inside and outside the office. Skill building individual development and professional training will help your employees meet their personal and career goals. Treat all your employees equally and make sure that each one has the chance to be promoted.

Be successful and reach what they want for their careers. When you prioritize their future you also validate their commitment to the organization and instill a strong sense of community and be flexible whenever possible. Offer a flexible working environment as long as hard work is also built into your company culture. Giving more freedom and flexibility can demonstrate that you trust your employees. In turn employees who benefit from these policies tend to be more loyal and committed to their jobs. Here are some initiatives to get you started with flexible working hours and lenient dress codes.

B y o d. Or bring your own device practice allowing employees to access social media platforms and messaging applications even during working hours, freedom to work off site or from home whenever your employees need to get away from the distractions of the office or get caught up on a project without getting frequently interrupted. Keep your employees safe. One of the hallmarks of a positive work culture is having the opportunity to speak openly about certain issues in and outside of the office. Ensuring that your employees know their rights are protected at work is just as essential as making sure they feel welcome. The following are examples of policies that you can initiate to make your employees feel safe H.R.

representatives should have enough time in their schedules to accommodate personal conversations when necessary implement an anonymous sexual harassment hotline which will serve as a secure and private way to report related incidents in the office don't sweep issues under the rug or shy away from tough conversations. A safe workplace isn't about avoiding conflict. Instead it requires facing problems head on before they become bigger issues, never making assumptions and asking open ended questions. This approach shows that you are open to whatever your employees have to say and adapt to different motivations.

Employees have motivations that vary depending on their age, expectations , experience and background.

For example a lot of senior employees tend to prefer having the flexibility and freedom to choose how they get their work done. On the other hand many younger employees like having short breaks during the workday to relax, play games, watch sports and just be able to get away for a few minutes from the daily grind. Figure out what motivates your employees and build it into your company culture. You want your employees to work hard and efficiently and this is only possible within a company culture that is hospitable to their interests and motivations. Creating a more positive and engaging organizational culture takes time, energy and dedication. You'll have to invest in significant and sustainable policy changes in order to realize the kind of work culture you desire.

Make sure that your key leaders are able to evolve with policy changes that are being implemented. They should understand their role in creating a culture that is aligned with the company's business strategy. They should also have goals and motivations that are congruent with the company's desired outcomes. Be inclusive. No one wants to feel uncomfortable at work because of their age, sexuality , gender ethnicity or any other important aspect of their being. Take the necessary steps to improve inclusion and diversity at the office. And don't make these policies into nothing more than lip service, implement them fully and have the necessary sanctions in place to penalize offenses.

Remember that even though there may be laws in place to prevent serious cases of workplace discrimination a working environment where events requiring legal intervention happen shouldn't exist in the first place. From the onset make it clear that the organization has a zero tolerance culture for workplace discrimination check accessibility if you have policies in place that are intended to promote the welfare, happiness and growth of your employees. Make sure that these policies are accessible for everyone. There is no point in having these policies if they'll only benefit a small group of people. While designing these policies. Keep in mind that people prefer and favor different things. For example when creating a recognition and rewards program.

Remember that some employees may prefer monetary rewards while others may want more vacation days. It's all about ensuring that everyone feels a sense of belonging and inclusion. Being open and transparent toxicity in a business environment can be very damaging. It hinders collaboration, suppresses new ideas and delays innovation. Create an open and transparent work environment where people won't be scared to express their thoughts and ideas no matter if they are an intern or a tenured senior employee. Employees are more productive and efficient when they feel like they can trust their leaders. Take the time to speak personally with all the people that directly report to you.

Develop a relationship that is based on mutual trust and respect so that your team members can speak freely without fear of backlash and be visible and accessible. Employees support leaders who are honest, transparent and authentic. When you make yourself available to everyone it creates a sense of unity and purpose. Employees are more likely to feel motivated to work hard to achieve company goals when they have leaders who strive to be a great role model for them. Be consistent. There are a lot of new trends in company culture that have become popular with both startups and larger corporations. It can be tempting to adopt these trends into your own organization to get the same benefits or to keep up with what your competitors are doing.

However remember that strategies and policies don't work the same way for every company. Instead of getting distracted by the newest business culture fad it might be best to stick with what is tried and tested. If you believe that you already have a terrific company culture where your employees thrive and are happy it's better to let things remain the same. While change is mostly a good thing. Disrupting what already works can be detrimental to your organization's cultural balance, constantly reiterating core values when you've already defined and institutionalized your company's core values. Make sure that you and your team are practicing and living these on a daily basis.

For instance during weekly meetings you can highlight core value leaders in the company and recognize their efforts and achievements. Furthermore be the change that you want to see, own and champion your company culture to remind people of its existence and importance. Hold yourself to the high standards called for by your company's values on a daily basis. Your team members will see your efforts and will be more likely to follow your example and make people feel valued. Everyone has a natural desire to be appreciated for their contributions and efforts. In fact the endeavor to demonstrate one's value can shape an employee's beliefs and attitudes at work to make sure that your employees feel like their work is valued and appreciated. Try the following tips.

Create a program that recognizes and rewards employee contributions. Don't let the efforts of your team go unnoticed if you want to retain their talent, improve productivity and sustain creative development. Let your employees know their contributions help the company achieve their overall goals. When employees understand how they affect the success of the company they take more pride in their work, ask for their feedback and opinions when applicable and let them know that their contributions are appreciated. Communicate frequently and efficiently to make sure that they are in the loop when it comes to important changes or updates within the organization.

Appreciate and empower. Studies show that while money is an important motivator, true motivation to perform well and produce good outcomes comes from appreciation and autonomy. When employees know that their work is meaningful and when they have a sense of purpose at work they make useful contributions. For this reason. Make sure that you offer the right feedback, support and resources that will empower your employees to do good work. Don't automatically assume that promotions and salary increases are the only ways you can raise an employee's status. Perception of status also rises when employees are appreciated by their employers and provide credible praise for daily tasks rather than waiting for them. End of the year performance evaluations increase engagement.

Make sure that your employees are in the loop about the latest updates in the company. They should be aware of the organization's future goals, plans for expansions and financials. Unless you are actively told to keep certain updates a secret it's better to have an open and transparent workplace to ensure continuous and productive engagement from the employees. A highly engaged workplace after all fosters a high performing workforce. Here are some ideas on how you can increase workplace engagement. Start activities that underscore social responsibility. This can involve volunteering for local animal shelters building homes or connecting with disadvantaged or underprivileged communities.

Create affinity or popular interest groups such as book clubs or a group where you can share pet tips and stories. Encourage your team to share more about themselves by creating spaces where they can comfortably talk about their hobbies and interests and plan regular company outings. These offer a great opportunity for your team to build bonds and new interpersonal connections outside of the office. Don't sacrifice your values for urgent demands. It's important to stay true to your values even in the face of urgent deadlines or demands. For example you may keep delaying one on one meetings because there's an urgent call or meeting that crops up every day.

However if you want to maintain a positive company culture make sure that you prioritize the things that are truly important for the company. It's okay to reschedule but don't let your company values such as your commitment to employee growth and development completely get replaced by the need to address urgent situations. Unless you maintain a regular connection with your company values you might find yourself having to deal with a decaying cultural fiber fostering creativity and innovation.

Make sure that you don't hinder your employees from innovating and creating by providing them with the support and resources they need. Here are some examples of the changes you can make to foster creativity and innovation redesign the office to encourage collaboration.

Consider getting standing desks to get people's minds sharp and engaged. Have a space where your team can relax and distress when they want to get away from the monotony of their desks. Encourage learning. One of the top reasons why employees leave a company is there is no room for growth in organized skill development Books, training sessions and coaching throughout the year to ensure that they are growing and improving, encouraging and opening offices where people can freely exchange ideas and hold regular meetings where everyone can participate. Set a good example by being receptive to every idea presented to you. Encourage freedom.

It's never a good idea to make employees feel that they're not involved in key decisions or that their impact on the company is insignificant when limited freedom becomes a part of your company culture. Your employees will feel that they're only helping someone else achieve their dreams. Make your employees feel that they have a voice and a meaningful impact on the organization and its direction. When people have ownership of their work the outcomes become more valuable to them. Encourage your employees to become stakeholders so that the company's success is directly tied to their efforts at work.

People feel proud when they are a part of something bigger than themselves, particularly when joint effort creates profitable outcomes, promotes camaraderie, builds a team that relies on each other, a positive close knit workplace culture boosts productivity, improves efficiency and increases the company's bottom line. Check out the following ideas on how you can promote camaraderie between your team members and plan company events so that the team has something to look forward to beyond the confines of the office. A casual gathering outside of the workplace enables people to get to know each other better and create friendships. Schedule a happy hour with your team and try out an escape room organized game day once a month. Remember that you don't have to break the bank to go on fun outings.

Don't prevent casual conversations during the day. In fact encourage them to connect on a deeper level with each other at work in many cases. Informal discussions can lead to creative ideas and exciting outcomes promote self care. Organizations that have thriving cultures prioritize the health and well-being of their employees. These companies understand that when employees are healthy and happy they bring their whole productive selves to work promoting self care also boosts company morale because people aren't stressed or pressured at work thus reducing health care costs try the following tips to cultivate a healthy environment at work. Encourage your employees to go for a short walk outside during the day.

Implementing a policy for gym membership reimbursements or discounts offer flexible work schedules or the choice to work remotely on occasion hold the fun and friendly challenges to get them away from their desks provide them information and resources on how they can reduce stress and protect the culture during the onboarding process. A candidate's disposition and attitude are crucial factors to consider. Negative people can bring down the entire workplace. So look for those with friendly and upbeat dispositions. Here are some ways to protect your company culture during expansion and change, be authentic and live up to your values. The lack of authenticity will be immediately discerned by your applicants, employees and customers.

Make sure they abide by company culture even when tough decisions or adverse changes inevitably occur. Be very public about your company culture. Reiterate it whenever possible including in the company handbook Web site office walls and promotional materials. This sends the message that you strongly believe in your values and won't be giving up on them anytime soon. Use your values as a recruitment tool. Applicants should be oriented by H.R. about the meaning of these values and whether or not these are the same values that they believe in carefully consider whether a candidate aligns with the company culture before they progress into the next steps in the hiring process.

Appointing mentors one effective way to bring culture into life is through mentorship. Match your more experienced employees with your new recruits. The former already have a deep understanding of the company culture and can play a considerable role in coaching the ladder mentors can help new recruits not just by teaching them what they need to know about the organization but by serving as living breathing examples of the company's core values allow for humor work can be very stressful and laughter can provide a much needed respite from the metronome of deadlines and revenue targets. Being able to see the lighthearted side of a tough situation is an important skill. While the ultimate goal is to get the problem resolved. Humor does offer some invaluable benefits.

After all, people rarely succeed unless they enjoy what they're doing. Laughter. According to research, it is not at odds with productivity. In fact people are more productive and better at problem solving when they're in a good mood. If you can find the bright side in difficult situations you can successfully cultivate a playful but creative working environment accepting and using feedback. The best way to start building a company culture is by asking your employees to share their thoughts and ideas. Remember that feedback isn't something you should fear. Instead of considering it as a sign that you're doing something wrong. Think of it as a way for the employees to show that they care about the company they're providing feedback to because they want to make the company better. Make sure that you also offer a way for your team members to provide feedback anonymously.

This will help them honestly share the things that they've been too shy or scared to say in person. There are digital surveys and feedback forms you can create for free to present yourself as a team. Every team has its star employees and underdogs. However if you want to build a positive company culture you shouldn't just focus on those individuals who are performing well. Instead make sure that your employees see themselves as part of a team. One success is the success of the entire team. And if there are any members who are lagging behind the team should work together to help bring them up to speed. When you present yourself as a team anyone can ask for help without worrying about whether they'll be criticized or judged.

Presenting yourself as a team is also more appealing to potential applicants to the company. It signals to outsiders that the employees and their leaders have a sense of belonging and that they hold each other in high regard. Put things in perspective. Encourage your team members to never lose sight of the bigger picture. They may encounter failures along the way but they should remember that there are plenty of other things that they should be proud of. Remind them that it's impossible to win at everything. Instead of blaming them for their mistakes they are going on an angry tirade.

Consider those mistakes as a learning opportunity fostering optimism creates a positive momentum in the workplace especially in times of conflict and strife when leaders and employees demonstrate an optimistic attitude during times of hardship. They'll create a productive mindset and a winning culture by investing in employee retention programs. The soaring employee turnover rate is a growing area of concern for employers recently. Most resumes today only feature one or two year stints at multiple companies. Studies show that employees are constantly on the hunt for better career opportunities.

High turnover rates are never a good thing for any company because it shows that employees are unhappy and it can also get very expensive to keep hiring and training new people. Here are some ways to increase employee retention. You should incorporate fair and routine pay raises so that your rates are competitive with other companies in the industry. Make sure that your employees are given opportunities for upward mobility. Many people who leave their jobs do so because of the lack of opportunity for career advancement to provide job security and stability. Frequent firings are whimsical decisions by the management that give workers the sense that they can be out of a job at any moment to improve office space. Open office spaces do not just help employers save money in space, they also foster collaboration and teamwork.

However they also don't work for all employees. Introverts for instance won't thrive in open working spaces where they are forced to give up their privacy instead of forcing this on all your employees to give them options. Let your employees create the kind of environment that would make them the most efficient and productive open spaces are great. But make sure that you also install several private rooms where employees can work without any distractions or interruptions. Celebrate cultural alignment and recognize employees or groups whose performance and subsequent success was guided by your company culture. Make sure to do this in a public setting and frame this milestone in such a way that supports the culture and values the organization upholds.

Furthermore, post this kind of achievement on your Web site so that potential employees can learn more about your culture and understand what achievements you value and recognize go easy on the dress code. A traditional dress code does offer some benefits. However if you wish to build a positive company culture consider opting for a more casual dress code in the workplace. Formal suits definitely create a rigid and uncomfortable environment. Most employees who don't have the right kind of clothes will also be forced to shop and spend money when employees feel comfortable. They perform better at work prioritizing comfort and productivity over image is a great way to engage your team.

Flexibility with the dress code also shows them that certain things don't matter as much as their happiness and performance. Modern technology advancements in technology have revolutionized the way that businesses operate. Most companies utilize platforms to improve communication, manage their work and streamline certain tasks. Integrate these platforms into your company when you are building a positive company culture. Technology can bring teams together and make their jobs a lot easier when your processes are more efficient in communication , collaboration and employee experience. Also significantly improve celebrating successes as a team. Teams that celebrate successes are also in a better position to deal with problems and challenges.

Don't hog the spotlight all to yourself if you have shared the responsibilities for a project. Make sure that you also share the recognition you received for successes and accomplishments when teams know that their efforts are appreciated. No matter how small a task seemingly is they are also more empowered to do their best and help others to do their best. After all, their teammates' success is also the success of the team and the entire organization. Articulate the need for change sometimes despite everyone's best efforts your company culture may not actually work. However you shouldn't just give up and consider the entire thing as a failure. Instead, think of it as an opportunity for growth and improvement to change your company culture and make it work for you.

Take note of four key practices that articulate your goals. Identify the problems with your existing culture and define what kind of culture you want. Instead find and develop leaders who align with the target culture. They will be able to help you achieve a new company culture by providing support, helping with strategy and passionately implementing policy changes using organizational conversations to emphasize why change is necessary at this point in time. Regular dialogue about the importance of a positive culture will help everyone realize the need for change.

Implement the changes by ensuring that the organization's processes systems and structures align with the new culture and now it's discussion time. The most important part of this training whoever is the head honcho in the group should designate a facilitator whose responsibility it is that each of the questions you see on your screen is covered and that everyone. Time permitting is able to have their say. Make sure all contributions are valued. All suggestions considered and all opinions respected.

Create High Performance Teams

Andrew Carnegie once said teamwork is the ability to work together toward a common vision. The ability to direct individual accomplishments toward organizational objectives. It is the fuel that allows common people to attain uncommon results. An organization's ability to succeed hinges on teamwork. The ability of your people to act together augment and accommodate each other's strengths , weaknesses and specialties is vital to the accomplishment of your mission. They must have a shared vision, shared focus and mutual trust. But how do you get your team to the point where they're able to embody these ideals?

How do you truly leverage the power of teamwork in the workplace? In this Book we're going to show you exactly how to do that. 86 percent of employers identified lack of collaboration or inefficient communication as the top cause of workplace failures. 97 percent of them also believe that a lack of team alignment adversely affects the outcome of a task or project. Fifty four percent of employees say that a strong sense of community at work helps them stay at a company longer based on those statistics. It seems like teamwork is an increasingly important area for businesses to focus on. This training is going to consist of a series of critical discussion points.

These are designed to cover this broad topic as thoroughly as possible to encourage growth in these vital areas and to facilitate a real and fruitful discussion within your organization about how you can each improve on this essential characteristic both at work and in your personal lives in general some of these will be pretty lengthy and some will be relatively straightforward in brief at the very end of this roadmap comes the most important final step discussion time. Do not skip this. This is the most important part of this training when you finish this Book. You need to spend at least an hour or so going over the questions we supply at the end.

As a group whoever is the head honcho in the group should designate a facilitator whose responsibility it is that each question is covered and that everyone time permitting is able to have their say. Make sure all contributions are valued. All suggestions considered and all opinions respected so let's move into the first discussion point clarify vision and goals. Your team should understand the purpose of the work they're doing unless they understand how their work contributes to the entire organization. Tasks and responsibilities can feel arbitrary or even directionless. The organization's vision for a project should be clearly communicated to the team so that they better understand the way you make decisions.

Make sure that your team also knows about the goals that they should be hitting and when set clearly defined and measurable goals within a specific timeframe to ensure that everyone's on the same page. This will make it easier for them to visualize where they stand relative to the designated benchmarks to communicate urgency. One of the biggest sources of workplace conflicts are misunderstandings about which tasks are most time sensitive. Make sure that your team knows which tasks are to win if there are urgent tasks that need to be attended to immediately make sure that everyone knows about them at the same time learn to distinguish urgencies that are best left for another day and emergencies where your team members should drop everything else and work on solving the issue.

This will help you avoid doing so much short sighted reactive work to the detriment of your key goals. Distributing tasks evenly teamwork doesn't mean you do one task together, rather teamwork involves breaking down a project into several attainable tasks. These tasks should then be divided among your team members. According to the following factors, the priority is to choose the person who can do the task as soon as possible without getting bogged down by other routine tasks. Find someone who can ensure high quality outcomes for the job because of their skills and expertise availability.

Pick the team member who has ample time and schedule to complete the work development. If you want a particular team member to upgrade their skills and increase their knowledge, give them tasks where they'll have to step up and learn interest. If someone is really interested about a specific task or responsibility let them take it on. Since their passion can motivate them to excel. Define roles clearly outline the roles of each member for every project. Everyone should be aware of the overall goals of the project but must also have their individual set of goals and tasks. When everyone knows what they're supposed to do they won't have to worry about stepping on someone else's toes when there is ambiguity regarding roles.

Your team won't be able to work together cohesively. Furthermore the confusion can lead to resentment. Make sure there is proper documentation for the roles assigned which should be accessible for your entire team. If there's any question regarding obligations your team can easily check this and avoid an escalation of conflict and divide roles based on individual strengths. Take a look at the skills of every single one of your team members and make sure that each one of them is placed where they can offer the most value identify their strengths and surround them with other people who can amplify and improve those strengths dividing roles and allocating tasks based on individual strengths isn't just about having the best person for the job but also creating an environment of success and achievement.

When someone knows that they're good at their job they'll feel valued and happy. This kind of positive energy will also radiate with the rest of the group to do lists to do lists, create order and remind your team which tasks they need to prioritize. Instead of writing daily To Do lists on sticky notes use a task management tool where task lists can be shared with the rest of the team. These apps and tools allow you to see pending and completed tasks so that everyone is up to date with the progress of a project shared to do lists. Also allow your team to have structure to their day, feel a sense of accomplishment when they're able to tick off an item on their list and manage their time better organized team processes more than just having clear goals and roles. You should also have definite team processes in place.

Your team should know what steps they should be following when working on projects mitigating setbacks communicating with each other and providing feedback well-defined team processes enable them to spend more time working and less time figuring out logistics consider adopting one of the popular project management methodologies listed below Agile is best suited for teams that need to increase productivity. It is specifically designed to provide teams with a definite measurable structure that encourages continuous development team collaboration and recognition scrum is often used for developing, delivering and sustaining complex products. It fosters collaboration accountability and repetitive progress can Ben helps build self managing and collaborative teams.

It aims to identify bottlenecks which are setbacks that can reduce the efficiency of a chain of processes and deliver high quality results. The lean methodology aims to reduce waste or inefficiencies. In order to create more value for clients and customers the Waterfall methodology is a traditional linear and sequential approach where progress moves in only one direction. It is ideal for projects in industries where structure is crucial for stringent and expensive stages or processes. The Six Sigma approach aims to enhance quality management by identifying what's causing errors and then removing it from the equation.

Rules help ensure that things work properly and effectively schedule a meeting where you can set the rules together as a team so that everyone can have a say in determining what will improve their productivity and efficiency. Deciding together will help them communicate, build trust and feel like their voices are being heard. Team rules are designed to provide everyone with a direction by making them work uniformly. Just make sure that rules don't hinder their individual growth. You shouldn't make rules so strict that it becomes difficult for an employee to work comfortably and independently improve meetings. A shared team calendar will help with making sure that everyone shows up on time for your meetings.

However if you don't run your meetings efficiently you're still going to lose a lot of time. After all, spending an hour with 10 people. Here are some ways to ensure that meetings boost team performance and productivity invite only the team members that need to be involved as much as possible. Send out meeting materials a day in advance so that everyone knows what they're supposed to do or prepare for. Make sure that you have a goal oriented agenda of the topics to be discussed and ensure that every meeting ends with definite resolutions set a time limit to discuss each issue when the time's up. Move on to the next issue immediately.

This will ensure that everyone contributes only their most relevant and important ideas, try non-traditional meeting formats such as walking or standing meetings to keep the attendees engaged and also ensure brevity build commitment. Make sure that every member of the team has a strong sense of commitment to the group. They should feel that their contributions will significantly impact the team's decisions and actions. Here are some tips to help make your team members feel more connected to their work and the team play up to their strengths. Make sure that each team member feels that they are bringing their best skills and ideas to the work they do.

When they know that they can be their best selves at work they'll feel more committed to what they do. Make sure that each one of them feels that their work is valuable to the team in the organization. Their role should help advance their career opportunities and attract positive attention to their capabilities. Make sure that they are excited and challenged by the opportunities that you send their way. Find tasks that are outside of their comfort zone and encourage them to step up and show the team what more they can bring to the table constantly improve the team should be able to constantly assess itself and find ways to enhance its practices processes and interactions spearhead regular discussions where the team can discuss any issues that may be hindering their growth and development as individuals and as a group.

Foster open and efficient communication everyone in the team should be able to openly communicate with both their superiors and their peers. They must have the opportunity to talk about their ideas and any challenges that may be hindering their progress. Take advantage of technology and create a virtual space where your team members can communicate and share ideas and brainstorm together. Ask and receive feedback and collaborate on tasks. Always keep in mind that good communication is the core of great teamwork. Building a feedback process feedback helps improve teamwork since it helps members identify where they're doing a great job and where they need some work, although it's important to give constructive criticism regularly. Make sure that your focus is on positive feedback.

It's a powerful tool to encourage a happy workplace and ensure that everyone feels valuable on top of providing feedback to the team as a whole. Organize individual assessment meetings for each one and your team. You can easily boost morale by providing timely feedback about the team's overall success and their individual contributions to that success solicit feedback.

It's crucial for the feedback process to be a two way street. You should always be open to feedback from your team. When you create an environment where your employees can openly share their ideas, comments and criticisms you promote trust and facilitate growth.

After all, when employees can easily provide feedback about the organization's policies and processes you can quickly make adjustments to ensure that you are doing things efficiently and effectively using a suggestion box if you are worried about any team member being too shy to offer up their ideas and concerns. You might want to create a platform for anonymous feedback. A virtual or physical suggestion box is an ideal tool for this, maintaining anonymity to generate new ideas offers distinct advantages. For instance brainstorming sessions may sometimes only produce contributions from people who are naturally outgoing or talkative.

Have as many feedback channels as possible to ensure that continuous flow of good ideas are recognized and rewarded when teamwork is considered as important as results. People will work actively to improve their skills and don't put the spotlight on people who may be performing well but are also working in isolation. Instead attach rewards and praise to successful outcomes that are achieved when the team works well together. Some examples are company or team white emails in person recognition tokens of appreciation. Extra vacation days bonuses and promotions.

Don't wait too long to recognize or reward your team for their good performance since the delay can breed resentment or a lack of confidence encourage brainstorming when you're working on a program schedule a brainstorming session at least weekly or bi monthly brainstorming sessions present the perfect opportunity for your team to think outside the box and come up with creative solutions welcome all ideas. Even the seemingly crazy ones when you listen to all the ideas that they put forward you create a culture where people feel comfortable sharing and talking at the same time you also empower them to be more confident.

Think creatively and develop a sense of ownership. Create clear timelines. Your team should have a clear picture of the schedule. Make sure that this schedule includes small milestones and individual goals so that they won't feel too pressured. Create a review routine to make sure that no one is falling behind. Nevertheless don't helm them too much. Provide support and tools for those individuals who are falling behind. For instance, I have a buddy system. So when some team members are done with their tasks they can provide assistance to those who are finding it difficult to complete. There's ongoing training. One way to boost your team's energy and morale is to ensure that they feel accomplished and valuable.

You can do this by ensuring that each team member gets the chance to develop and improve their skills through ongoing training designed or sponsored by the management development Books and training sessions will boost your team's knowledge and improve their performance. Remember that training doesn't have to be limited to technical skills. You can also schedule training Books for social or leadership skills as well as other aptitudes that will make them more effective in the workplace and unlock creativity no matter how technical your industry may be. Creativity and innovation are always welcome.

Creativity fuels solutions for complex problems and meeting the needs of customers and clients. Your team is composed of creative people with a diverse range of experience and knowledge tapping into this resource will help you get the most out of collaboration and encourage your team members to share their ideas and opinions. Ban negative comments such as what a stupid idea from the entire office when you have brainstorming sessions. Judgment should be left at the door. Nurture an environment that welcomes new and fresh ideas. Implement the buddy system. Try a buddy system where you pair new employees with those who have been in the company for a year or more.

The veterans will help the newbies with the onboarding process and answer questions regarding the work of the people and the company. They'll also help them with learning and embracing the company culture. A buddy system won't just help new hires learn the ropes. It will also help forge bonds that will last beyond the onboarding period. Most buddy pairs will learn each other's work styles intimately and become more effective collaborators later on to improve the workspace. Your office space should be conducive for the growth of teamwork. You'll have to find ways to change the physical workspace so that it actively supports collaboration Some examples are the following allocate project and conference rooms that have remote conferencing tools which your team can use when collaborating create spaces that encourage impromptu huddles for productive discussions and provide accessibility to other team members.

Make sure that you also have space for people to work alone and finish their tasks in peace. The job may get done more quickly as a team but individuals should still be able to use their personal time to focus and work peacefully. Studies have found that open plan layouts for offices can help level hierarchies in the office and promote more collaboration within the team. Consider the benefits of implementing hot desks, shared spaces, flexible spaces or huddle areas to boost flexibility and collaboration. Have a centralized space to make sure that all the projects and tasks that your team is working on are under one roof.

A centralized space where you can manage the workload will help prevent things from getting messy and mixed up. This is also crucial if you have team members that are located in different offices or who work remotely a project management software platform or app will make it easier for your team to see all the relevant project data. Determine which tasks are assigned to whom. Any updates on their progress and how much work still needs to be done. Set healthy boundaries. Although it's ideal to have a collaborative and harmonious work environment it's still crucial to set healthy boundaries. For instance, anyone in your team should be free to refuse talking about their personal lives.

They shouldn't be pressured into joining late night activities with their colleagues if they believe that it will interfere with their productivity at work and teach your team the importance of respecting each other's limitations and boundaries. At the same time encourage them to communicate about their limits to the rest of the team. Very clearly if any boundaries are violated let them know that they are free to speak up and reinforce these limits in the moment take breaks together according to research teams that take breaks together demonstrate a higher level of productivity getting together in an informal setting encourages communication and bonding between the team try to round up your team every week to grab a coffee together.

You can also buy some sweets for the morning huddle. Try having a walking team meeting. Nothing brings people closer and boosts their willingness to work together than stepping away from work to enjoy a good old break. Post company functions as a great way to help your team. Bond is the host of social events or company functions no matter how big or small you want it to be. This is a great way to boost morale and camaraderie among the members. Some examples are the following: post an awards ceremony, post a potluck where everyone can bring in their favorite dish by your team, lunch and dinner, or you can check out a restaurant in the area and have some happy hour drinks after business hours to get to know each other better and improve team rapport. Whole team building activities and formal team building activities have their benefits.

They ensure participation and promote team spirit, trust and support for each other. However, forcing people to participate in compulsory team building activities can be detrimental to teamwork. You want to avoid resentment from festering so don't impose these activities like a ruthless dictator instead encourage organic and informal team building activities. These are done in low pressure settings where your team can get to know each other better and form bonds that will extend to the office exercise together if you have gym facilities in the building or if there is one located near the office. Consider scheduling simple exercises and workouts at least once a month with your team.

Exercise won't just improve your team's health it will also help boost their morale and team spirit. Arrange for yoga stretching or light cardio sessions for the team. Since these are easy and simple exercises that anyone can participate in to start team traditions, traditions bring people together and instill a sense of solidarity and camaraderie. If you want to encourage a unified culture in your team. Starting traditions that everyone can understand or participate in some examples are the following. A running inside joke incentives or celebrations for achievements and successes annual retreats into tropical destinations bringing snacks or homemade food.

On a specific day of the week schedule an annual summit consider holding an annual summit where everyone can have their say in improving company mission and goals. This will also give everyone the chance to take a step back from the daily stress of work and participate in some fun activities with the rest of the team. An annual summit will encourage teamwork and collaboration because it brings the entire organization together to remember what they are all working for. Hold sessions or workshops where groups from different departments can get together to brainstorm on one topic and mediate disputes. You should have a process in place to immediately address and resolve issues that arise among team members.

When team members understand how they remedy their problems without any negative effects they'll be more empowered to solve their issues productively and efficiently. Keep in mind that when conflicts are not resolved quickly they can damage Internal Relations, create divisions within the group and cause a breakdown of communication in time they'll slow work down and adversely affect the organization's overall output. Prioritizing diversity, most employers typically Group employees with certain things in common such as their background skills or personality. Sometimes this can be unconscious especially because some pairings just seem to make more sense. In most cases homogeneous teams work because it is easier for them to get along and work with each other.

However diverse groups often lead to a more productive collaboration. Diverse teams allow their members to think creatively and come up with solutions from different perspectives, promote diversity in your team and challenge yourself to mix up groupings with every new project or opportunity for collaboration. Challenge the status quo and get your employees out of their comfort zones. Have an open door policy. One of the biggest problems that employees face is finding a way to communicate with their bosses and managers. They may not feel comfortable with approaching the higher ups directly as a result.

Their work may suffer and important points and ideas may never get brought up open door policies are meant to encourage your team members to offer suggestions and ideas or seek advice and counsel when they're facing some roadblocks with their work having an open door policy at your office creates an environment of mutual respect and trust where your team can feel comfortable bringing their issues to your attention at any time use collaboration tools make sure that your team has the necessary resources to communicate with each other effectively and efficiently. Here are some examples of collaboration tools that facilitate a more efficient working environment.

Comfortable workspaces which the team can use to discuss their tasks or brainstorm if the team needs to communicate with other departments in different locations. You should have remote working tools such as video conferencing, use an online collaboration and communication portal to get things organized and improve access to each other. Use Project Management apps that automatically remind each team member about their tasks. Deadlines and priorities promote autonomy. You should empower your team to understand the project and organization goals and act autonomously to accomplish these goals. Put the decision and control in their hands instead of micromanaging them.

Remember that micromanagement shows your lack of trust in their skills and cripples your team's ability to manage their own work. Here are some great tips to help encourage your team to be more autonomous at work: ask for their input and act on their feedback. Let the team set their deadlines and only check in if you have a valid reason to be concerned. Let them set their own schedule especially with deliverables and ask for their ideas when designing team and organizational processes. Offer them plenty of opportunities to step up more and develop new skills, encourage transparency, and make sure that everyone can see what everyone else is doing. It's more difficult for team members to lend a hand to their colleagues when they don't know what they're doing or which part they're having difficulties with.

Transparency with work responsibilities make it easier for any team member to help out when needed or collaborate for certain tasks encourage your team to part ways with personal spreadsheets or notepads for tracking their work. Instead ask them to use a shared spreadsheet or task management tool where tasks are easily visible to everyone else. This would also allow you to see what they're currently working on how much of their time each task consumes their output and which tasks are pending allow work flexibility teamwork thrives in a setting where every team member feels like they're trusted to do their work skillfully and effectively recent studies point out growing evidence that more employees prefer working outside of the traditional office hours being able to work whenever it is most convenient improves work life balance as well as their productivity allowing your team to be more flexible with their working hours demonstrates your trust in their capabilities.

Just make sure that you have a way to track the work they put in and a process to evaluate their performance if you're unsure whether it is the right choice for the organization. Consider testing it out for a month or giving your team members one day in the week when they could work remotely and don't rely on overtime most of the time. Teams that don't know what everyone else is working on will keep on working until everything in their task list for the day gets cleared out in many cases. This will lead to overtime. The problem with overreliance on overtime is that it becomes everyone's go to solution in any situation that goes slightly out of the norm instead of depending too much on overtime.

Get a clearer picture of how each member is spending their time. This doesn't mean policing their time. Rather it involves establishing how much work your team is doing. How much time each task takes and redistributing work when necessary. Plan together teamwork begins when your team fully supports your vision and goals. If the first time they hear about our plan is when they're getting a list of assignments from you. It's easy for them to have misgivings about what the end goal is really meant to accomplish, start sharing and collaborating from the moment you start planning. Ask them to weigh in on your ideas and express any misgivings they may have. Let them have their say about the projects they work on instead of applying your decisions unilaterally.

This simple step at the beginning of each year or quarter will help them be more excited about the upcoming work higher together and consider making the onboarding process a team responsibility. If you are planning to add someone new to the team to help out with the workload he lists your team's opinions and ideas before you make the final decision. This is important not just because your team will feel that their opinions are valued and respected but also because adding even just one new person can significantly impact the overall dynamics of your team it's beneficial to have your team have their say on who will be the best fit for them constantly challenged the team growth and development doesn't need to be restricted to the specific industry you are in.

You can also challenge your team with problems that are not related to certain projects or tasks but would improve their ability to work together and build better problem solving skills. Some good examples are solving giant puzzles or murder mysteries. These small problems would require the team to communicate, collaborate and have fun during the workday. It's a chance for them to experiment with various solutions and work together as a team track and measure. Remember that you can improve something that can't be measured.

Keep your eye on the metrics to ensure that your team is performing the way you want them to constantly check and assess any changes in sales income productivity and even staff retention rates. If you're seeing bad numbers then maybe it's time to bring in some much needed improvements. Use tactics that would help enhance communication and collaboration. Otherwise if the trend is mostly positive scale your efforts practice participative leadership give everyone in the team a chance to lead. This would give everyone the opportunity to actively contribute in being directly responsible for the team's successful outcomes and projects. Here are some roles that you can give a member of your team.

Every now and then leading meetings listening down decisions and commitments and reminding those who made them. Assigning tasks holding other team members accountable providing direction for the team eliminates access. Employees can get bogged down by small repetitive tasks that take up a lot of their time. These tasks can adversely impact teamwork especially if they're only being done by one or a few members of the team. Find ways to automate these tasks so that they can spend more time on bigger and more important tasks. At the very least try to distribute tasks like these evenly so that it's not just one member of your team taking care of all these tedious tasks. Minimize the importance of rank and let each team member no matter their position or seniority in the team.

Take part in the decision making process. Doing this will make them feel integral to the team's success and will do wonders for their morale. Instead of focusing on rank and giving all the crucial responsibilities to those who have a higher rank or have been there longer, take advantage of the entire group's talents. Keep the balance of work equal and the distribution of roles dependent on each one's strengths and skills spot red flags. Watch out for red flags of poor or failing group dynamics. If your team is unable to work together cohesively it could prevent the organization from achieving its goals and individual employees from reaching their true potential.

Here are some of the top warning signs that there has been a breakdown in teamwork: frequent unanimous decisions can be a sign of free riding, bullying or groupthink. Consider finding new ways for the team to discuss their ideas and opinions. If you consistently get results that are different from what is expected or planned it may show that people are having trouble communicating with each other or understanding what is required of them. When people frequently blame each other for mistakes it's a sign that they don't trust each other. Cultivating trust by encouraging them to spend more time with other people outside of their usual crowd work duplication shows that employees are unsure about what other members of the team are responsible for.

Using more transparent project management or task assignment tools to prevent this and ensure that everyone knows what they should be working on overreliance on indirect communication can also be a problem. Emails and texts are a convenient way to communicate but when you are in the same office direct face to

face communication is ideal. And now it's discussion time. The most important part of this training whoever is the lead honcho in the group should designate a facilitator whose responsibility it is that each of the questions you see on your screen is covered and that everyone time permitting is able to have their say. Make sure all contributions are valued. All suggestions considered and all opinions respected.

www.ingramcontent.com/pod-product-compliance
Lightning Source LLC
Chambersburg PA
CBHW071949210526
45479CB00003B/866